penguins

penguins

BY RICHARD TENAZA

FRANKLIN WATTS

NEW YORK | LONDON
TORONTO | SYDNEY | 1980

A FIRST BOOK

Photographs by Richard Tenaza on pages
3, 6, 7, 8, 19, 22, 23, 26, 28, 29, 32, 42, and 53.

Photographs courtesy of Seaworld
facing page 1, and on pages 15 and 48.

Photographs courtesy of Hanna-Barbera's
Marineland on pages 10 and 36.

Photographs courtesy of the Zoological Society
of London on pages 18 and 34.

Map design by Vantage Art, Inc.

Cover photograph by Richard Tenaza

Library of Congress Cataloging in Publication Data

Tenaza, Richard.
Penguins.

(A First book)
Bibliography: p.
Includes index.
SUMMARY: Introduces the physical characteristics,
behavior, and natural environment of various spe-
cies of penguins.
1. Penguins — Juvenile literature.
[1. Penguins] I. Title.
QL696.S473T45   598.4'41   79-22138
ISBN 0-531-04104-2

contents

INTRODUCTION
1

GETTING ABOUT
2

PENGUIN FOODS
9

PREDATORS OF PENGUINS
11

FOOD CHAINS
12

KEEPING WARM
13

COOLING OFF
16

ACQUIRING NEW FEATHERS
17

BREEDING
20

THE LANGUAGE OF PENGUINS
40

UNUSUAL PENGUINS
41

FOSSIL PENGUINS
43

COMFORT MOVEMENTS
44

FIGHTING
45

PENGUINS AND HUMANS
46

EPILOGUE
52

BIBLIOGRAPHY
55

INDEX
57

FOR LAURIE AND AMY

Acknowledgments
I thank Lorraine and Lanore Hirsch for their encouragement and Sarah Schilling for typing the manuscript. The U.S. National Science Foundation, the U.S. Antarctic Research Program, and Drs. J. T. Emlen and D. H. Thompson made my observations of penguins in Antarctica possible. Sea World in San Diego provided me with the opportunity to observe several species of penguins in captivity.

penguins around the world

Galapagos
(Galapagos Islands)

Peruvian
(Peru)

King
(South Georg
Island)

Sclater
(Aukland Island)

Humboldt
(Ocean current)

Gentoo
(Falkland Islands)

Thick-billed
(New Zealand)

Magellan
(Cape Horn)

Rockhopper
(Falkland Islands)

White-flippered
(New Zealand)

Chinstrap
(S. Orkney Islands)

Emperor
(Palmer Peninsula)

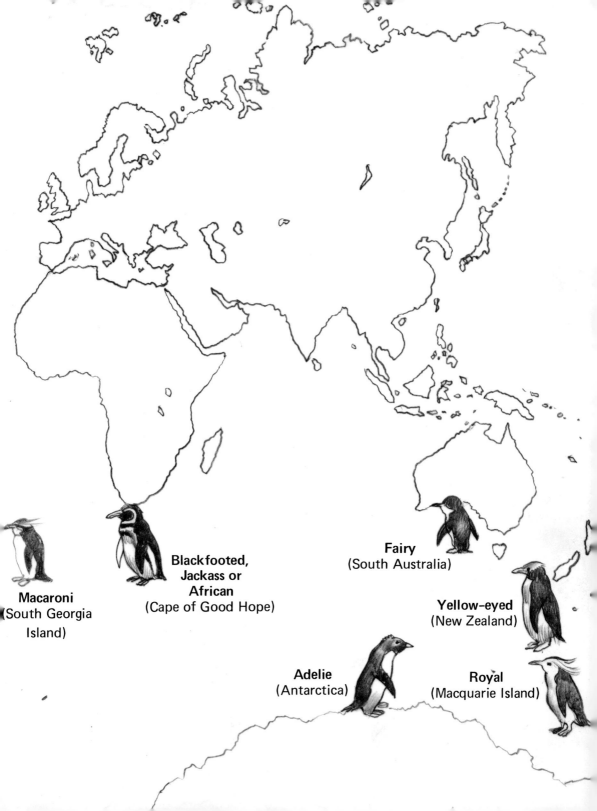

Macaroni
(South Georgia
Island)

**Blackfooted,
Jackass or
African**
(Cape of Good Hope)

Fairy
(South Australia)

Yellow-eyed
(New Zealand)

Adelie
(Antarctica)

Royal
(Macquarie Island)

penguins

**Emperor
Penguins**

introduction

The upright posture, waddling gait, armlike flippers, and black and white feathered exterior of penguins make them look more like humans dressed in formal attire than like the feathered creatures of the sea they are. That probably is why penguins are among the most appealing and popular birds in the world.

Penguins have been known for many hundreds of years to native inhabitants of southern Africa, South America, Australia, and New Zealand. However, they were not discovered by Europeans until late in the fifteenth century. At that time Portuguese sailors on a voyage of exploration rounded the Cape of Good Hope, at the southern tip of Africa, and encountered black-footed penguins. Since then, eighteen different kinds, or species, have been discovered and named by scientists. Most of them live south of the equator — that is, in the earth's southern hemisphere. One species, the Galapagos penguin, inhabits the Galapagos Islands, right on the equator. The others live further south, where they breed on islands and along the coasts of South America, southern Africa, Antarctica, Australia, and New Zealand. Penguins range in size from the little fairy penguin, standing 14 inches (35 cm) tall and weighing about 2 pounds (.9 kg), to the emperor penguin, which is more than 3 feet (1 m) tall and weighs 55 to 100 pounds (24 to 45 kg).

Even before the European discovery of the birds we now call penguins, the term *penguin* appeared in the English language. It referred to another type of large, upright, flightless bird, the great auk. These magnificent black and white birds were once widespread and abundant in the North Atlantic Ocean. They inhabited

(1)

coastal areas of northern Europe and northeastern North America. On land the great auk was clumsy and easy to capture, much as real penguins are. Unfortunately for them, their meat and eggs were edible, and they were hunted and egged to extinction. The last great auks on earth were killed in 1844 by hunters on an island near Iceland. Before they disappeared, great auks were well known to sailors in the North Atlantic. It is very likely that a sailor familiar with the great auk, or "penguin," was responsible for transferring the name to the birds we now call penguins.

getting about

Penguins, unlike other birds, cannot fly through the air. A penguin's wings are just too small to support its heavy body in the air. This is because the feathers on a penguin's wings are small, resembling fish scales more than they do the long wing feathers of flying birds.

Penguins would have little to gain by flying in air, however. The ability to fly in air is useful for seeking food, for avoiding enemies, and for migrating long distances. But penguins live where their food is available all year long and where they have relatively few natural enemies. Also, the distances they migrate are very short compared to those of many flying birds. Hence penguins have abandoned flight, and have been able to adapt more fully to life in the water as a result.

However it is not entirely true that penguins cannot fly. In water they use their paddle-like wings to push themselves along exactly the way other birds do in air. Considered this way, penguins do fly, but they do it in water rather than in air. Penguins flying underwater flap their wings about two times each second,

Adelie penguins "flying" in water.

the same rate that most birds flying in air flap theirs. The webbed feet of penguins, placed far back on their bodies, are used for steering as the penguin flies through the water.

Although penguins may appear comical and clumsy when walking, in the water they are quick and powerful swimmers. Their bodies are tapered at both ends, much like a torpedo or a jet plane. This streamlined shape helps them move smoothly through the water. The same kind of shape also aids the movement of other fast swimming animals such as tuna, seals, and dolphins.

Penguins eat shrimp, fish, and squid that they capture while diving beneath the surface of the sea. How deep do they dive in their search for food? Scientists have learned that penguins usually do not dive deeper than 70 feet (21 m). An emperor penguin was observed going down to nearly 900 feet (270 m), but such deep dives are very rare. During their dives penguins usually stay underwater for less than three minutes, then they swim to the surface and breathe before diving again. Sometimes, but not often, a penguin may stay underwater for as long as eighteen minutes.

One peculiar thing about penguins that helps them to get underwater is that their bones are solid and heavy, compared to the very light, hollow bones of flying birds. Some penguins even swallow pebbles, which may make diving easier because it makes the penguin's body heavier.

While moving through water penguins often use a kind of swimming known as *porpoising*. When porpoising, a penguin alternates between swimming rapidly underwater for a short distance then leaping forward through the air, breathing while out of the water. The famous biologist George Gaylord Simpson believes that porpoising may save energy because once the penguin has leapt out of the water it moves through the air without having to work as it does when swimming. Another possible advantage of porpoising is that a penguin is able to spot enemies such as killer whales or leopard seals farther away than it could if it did not leap up out of the water, and this may give the penguin a better chance of escaping these predators.

Adelie and emperor penguins in Antarctica are faced with the problem of having to get out of the sea onto steep, slippery ice floating on the sea's surface. They solve this problem by diving down beneath the surface, then swimming upwards very rapidly and with such force that they shoot up out of the water and land on the ice. A friend of mine, Dr. Gerald Kooyman of Scripps Institute for Oceanography, nearly lost an eye thanks to this practice. He was leaning over a hole in the ice observing penguins below when suddenly a large emperor penguin broke water, intent on leaping out onto the ice. The penguin's sharply pointed bill struck Dr. Kooyman's face just an inch from his eye. Luckily both Dr. Kooyman and the penguin survived the accident without permanant damage.

On ice and land penguins usually walk or run in the typical upright posture that makes them look so much like little men. However, when they are moving on ice or snow penguins often use another means of locomotion known as *tobogganing*. To toboggan, a penguin lies with its chest down and pushes with its feet and flippers to send itself gliding smoothly over the ice like a person on a sled or toboggan. On smooth ice or snow penguins can travel faster by tobogganing than they can by walking. Penguins travel at 2 to 3 miles (3.2 to 4.8 km) an hour when walking and up to 8 miles (12.8 km) per hour tobogganing. Normal walking speed for a person is about 3 miles (4.8 km) per hour.

Penguins have often been observed walking in single file over ice or land. This game of follow the leader seems to have great benefit for the followers. The first penguin in the line beats a path through the loose snow. The followers can then stay on this path rather than work to make a new one.

(5)

At left: an adelie will leap out of
the water onto the slippery sea ice.
Above: adelies can travel faster by
tobogganing over sea ice than by walking.

A group of adelies on Possession Island returning
to their colony in their typical single-file fashion.

Adelie penguins nest at the same seaside locations during the Antarctic summer year after year, although they may spend the winter on the pack ice hundreds of miles away. Scientists, curious about the ability of these birds to find their way home, captured adelies at their nests and moved them more than 1,000 miles (1,600 km) by plane before releasing them. Most of the displaced penguins returned to their nest sites the following year. The scientists later discovered that penguins find their way about the icy continent and seas of Antarctica by using the sun as a compass. On clear, sunny days adelie penguins can tell direction quite well. But on very cloudy days, when the sun is hidden from view, they have difficulty. Fortunately for the adelies, during the Antarctic summer, when they must find their nesting colonies again, the sun is in the sky for nearly twenty-four hours each day. Several other species of penguins also migrate but less is known about how they find their way.

penguin foods

Penguins obtain all of their food from the sea. They eat fish, squid, cuttlefish, and a variety of crustaceans, including shrimp, crabs, and lobster. As far as Antarctic penguins are concerned, the most important crustaceans are small, slow-swimming, shrimplike animals known as euphausiid shrimp, or krill. Dense aggregations of krill swarm about near the surface of the Antarctic seas, where they form more than ninety percent of the diet of adelie penguins. Krill are also eaten extensively by emperor penguins and are the main food of the gigantic Antarctic blue whale, which filters millions of these tiny organisms from the sea with its enormous mouth.

A Peruvian penguin.

Not all penguins are so highly dependent on krill as the adelie is. For example, Galapagos and Peruvian penguins feed mainly on small fishes, while the principal food of the Magellanic penguin in Argentina is squid. Emperor penguins eat crabs, cuttlefish, squid, and fish in addition to krill.

Krill and other penguin foods are salty. Furthermore, penguins usually have only salt water to drink (though they will drink fresh water when it is available). Because of this, penguins would build up toxic, or poisonous, levels of salt in their bodies if they had no way to get rid of the excess. Penguins, and many other seabirds, have solved this problem with special structures called salt glands, which are located beneath the skin on each side of the head above the eyes. These glands remove salt from the blood and concentrate it into a solution that is transported by little ducts to the bird's nose, where it drips off the bill and is lost.

predators of penguins

Animals that capture and eat (or prey upon) members of other species are called *predators* of those species. For example, adelie penguins are predators of krill, robins are predators of earthworms, and mountain lions are predators of deer. Just as penguins prey on krill, squid, and other forms of life, penguins themselves are hunted by other predators.

Leopard seals, fur seals, and sea lions are among the animals that prey on penguins in the water. In the seas around the continent of Antarctica leopard seals kill more penguins than do any other predator. Scientists have found as many as eighteen adelie penguins in the stomach of a single leopard seal. These large seals hide in the sea below the ice and wait for penguins to jump in. No penguin, consequently, is anxious to be the first to enter the water. After the first penguin dives in, the others peer over the edge of the ice. If no leopard seal has attacked, the others will then dive in. Further north, fur seals and sea lions replace the sea leopard as the chief predators of penguins. Killer whales, blue sharks, and giant petrels also capture penguins in the water on occasion.

Penguins appear to have more predators on land than they do in the sea. In Antarctica, gull-like birds known as skuas are major predators of eggs and chicks, though they are no match for a healthy adult penguin. In Australia, tiger snakes, large lizards, gulls, sea eagles, foxes, house cats, and water rats eat penguin eggs, chicks, and occasionally, adults. In South Africa the sacred ibis is an additional predator of penguins' eggs and chicks. Octopuses in South Africa capture penguin chicks entering the sea for the first time. In the Galapagos Islands the sally light-foot crab consumes eggs and deserted chicks of penguins. Hawks, rats, dogs, and cats also capture Galapagos penguins.

food chains

We have seen that penguins eat some organisms and in turn are eaten by others. In other words, penguins fit into what biologists call *food chains*. Green plants are the basis of nearly all food chains. Using energy from the sun, green plants are able to convert water and the gas carbon dioxide into material the plant can use. To complete this process, called photosynthesis, plants require additional nutrients such as calcium, phosphorus, sulphur, sodium, magnesium, and certain other chemical elements. The green plants important in penguin food chains are tiny one-celled organisms called phytoplankton. (*Phyto* refers to plants and *plankton* refers to or-

(12)

ganisms that are moved about in the sea more by wind and currents than by their own power.) In the case of the adelie penguin's food chain, the phytoplankton are eaten by krill, which are planktonic animals. Any phytoplankton, penguin, or other organism that dies in the sea is ultimately eaten or decomposed by microorganisms such as bacteria. Through this process the remains of dead plants and animals are broken down into chemical elements that can be used again by phytoplankton.

keeping warm

Penguins, like all birds, are warm-blooded. They normally maintain a body temperature of 100 to 102° Fahrenheit (38 to 39° Centigrade), which is even higher than our own normal temperature of 98.6° Fahrenheit (37° Centigrade). Even during February, which is the warmest month of the year in Antarctica, the Antarctic sea surface heats up to only about 41°F (5°C), and air temperatures might reach about 42 to 46°F (6 to 8°C) during the warmest hours of the warmest day. In winter, air temperatures around the coast of Antarctica drop to 40° below zero on both the Fahrenheit and Centigrade scales, and the sea is always slightly below 32°F (0°C), that is, below the freezing point for fresh water. A human cannot survive more than ten minutes in such cold water, but penguins seem comfortable swimming in it for hours. In the rest of this chapter, we will explore the ways penguins have found to keep themselves warm, even when the temperatures surrounding them are so cold.

The two major problems warm-blooded animals have in keeping warm are, first, they must produce heat and, second, they must conserve, or keep from losing, the heat that they produce.

Actually all animals, even cold-blooded ones, produce heat during normal chemical activities of the body (called *metabolism*). Warm-blooded animals are warm-blooded because they have ways to keep metabolic heat in their bodies rather than losing it to the outside environment.

Feathers and fat are two very important means that penguins use to stay warm. Feathers work by trapping a warm layer of air around the penguin's body. Air trapped in the feathers, or plumage, is kept warm by the penguin's metabolic heat. Your clothing works in the same way, trapping air warmed by your body's metabolism around you. Penguins even have a kind of "long underwear" formed by soft, fluffy feather tufts lying close to the body, beneath the outer clothing of windproof, waterproof feathers. Adelie penguins have feathers over their nostrils. These help to warm the cold air the birds must breathe. They also keep snow from entering a bird's nose.

Fat, or blubber, of penguins provides additional insulation. It forms a thick layer surrounding the body just beneath the skin. Because blubber is a poor conductor of heat, it helps to keep heat in the body instead of conducting it to the skin, where it can be lost. As you might have guessed, tropical penguins have thinner plumage and thinner fat layers than polar species.

Although the bodies of penguins are well-insulated with feathers and fat, their feet and flippers are not. When outside temperatures are well below freezing, the temperature of a penguin's feet and flippers may drop to 32°F (0°C), just barely above the point at which they will freeze. Nonetheless, blood from the interior of the penguin's body must flow out to these extremities to provide them with oxygen and nourishment.

How does the penguin avoid losing heat when its warm blood is sent out to nourish its cold extremities? The answer is really quite simple: Each blood vessel (artery) carrying warm blood into

**The Gentoo penguin is kept warm partly by
its feathers, which lie close to its body.**

the penguin's flipper, or foot, is surrounded by several other vessels (veins) that transport cold blood from the extremity back into the body. Heat is exchanged in these vessels, so that the cold blood returning to the body is warmed and the warm blood entering the extremity is cooled. The result is that very little heat is lost from the penguin. This is called a *countercurrent heat-exchange system*.

All penguins have black backs, which they are able to use in a special way to help them keep warm, at least when the sun is shining. Different hues have different abilities to absorb heat energy from the sun. Black absorbs heat more efficiently than any other shade. White, on the other hand, reflects heat. That is why if you place a black object and a white object next to one another in bright sunlight, the black one will heat up much faster than the white. Penguins can take advantage of this by turning their backs to the sun when they need to warm up. By the same token, a penguin that is in danger of overheating can face the sun with its white front and deflect much of the sun's heat.

Emperor penguins incubate their eggs on Antarctic sea ice during the cold, dark Antarctic winter. To conserve body heat in such extremely cold weather, emperor penguins incubating their eggs crowd up against one another to form tight bunches called huddles. A huddle may contain as many as 6,000 emperor penguins. Chicks of some of the other penguin species also form huddles, but the emperor penguin is the only kind in which the adults huddle.

cooling off

Strange as it may seem, penguins sometimes need to cool off. This is especially true of penguins living in warm regions such as the

Galapagos Islands. But it also applies to penguins in Antarctica during the summer.

The main problem is caused by heat absorbed from the sun, particularly during the nesting season. In the Galapagos, Argentina, and other warm areas, most penguins simply avoid the hot sun by nesting underground, either in natural caverns or in burrows that they dig themselves.

Penguins can cool off by ruffling up their body feathers. This exposes bare skin to the air. Even in the tropical Galapagos Islands, on the equator, the air is nearly always cooler than a penguin's normal body temperature. Penguins can also allow warm blood to flow into their flippers and feet, where it is cooled before returning to the main body. Another way penguins can stop themselves from becoming overheated in hot weather is by panting.

acquiring new feathers

Penguins grow their first set of feathers while still in the egg. By the time they hatch, penguin chicks have a complete coat of gray down feathers. These soft, fluffy, baby feathers are eventually replaced by stiff, sleek, water-repellent adult feathers which grow in beneath, pushing the baby feathers out. This process by which birds lose old feathers and grow new ones is called *molting*. The age at which the molt from baby down to adult-type feathers occurs is about seven weeks in adelie penguins and four to five months in emperor penguins. But in king penguins this molt does not occur until the chicks are nearly a year old or even older. Young penguins cannot enter the sea before their baby down is replaced by these waterproof feathers.

Adult penguins molt once a year. This is necessary because

Left: Humboldt's penguins, native to
warm western South America,
cool off by ruffling their feathers.
Above: an adelie chick is born with a
complete coat of gray down feathers.

the feathers wear out as they are used and they need replacement. The molt begins at the end of the breeding season. Before molting, a bird goes to sea and feeds until it is quite fat. It then hauls out on land or on floating sea ice to molt. Molting takes from two to five weeks, some species requiring more time than others. As the new feathers grow in the old ones are pushed out. When large patches of feathers fall out at the same time, the penguin may be left looking quite naked over parts of its body. Penguins do not eat at all during this period. Energy to generate new feathers and to keep the penguin alive is derived from the fat stored up before the molt. By the time molting is completed the penguin has lost 40 to 50 percent of its body weight and is very thin. However, a penguin entering the sea to feed before its molt is completed would risk dying of exposure to the cold water.

breeding

The life cycles of the eighteen species of penguins are all variations on a common theme. An egg is fertilized, laid, and incubated for a month or more until the baby penguin, which has been developing within the egg, breaks out of it. The penguin chick is then fed and cared for by both its parents for several weeks or months until it is able to fend for itself. The "adolescent" penguin spends from two to six years maturing before it finally seeks a mate and begins a family life of its own.

ADELIE PENGUINS
We will examine the adelie penguin here in detail because it is a species I have studied personally, firsthand in Antarctica.
Winters in Antarctica are not only long and cold, they are

dark as well. For half of the year the sun scarcely rises. During this prolonged winter darkness the adelies live at sea. When they are not in the water fishing or swimming, they can be found perched out on the floating, freezing pack ice. Their adaptations for keeping warm are put to good use here!

As the days lengthen into spring, the adelies get restless until finally, in late September or early October, they start moving in groups back toward their breeding grounds. No one knows for sure exactly how far any particular penguin must migrate to reach its nesting ground, but in some cases the distance must be very far indeed. Of that we are certain, because the southernmost adelie colony, located at Cape Crozier in the Ross Sea, is well over 500 miles (800 km) from its nearest wintering area.

There are vast stretches of shoreline in Antarctica where adelie penguins do not nest at all. In fact, they nest only in very local areas which we refer to as breeding grounds, or *rookeries*. Rookeries vary in size from small ones, with only a few hundred birds, to large ones containing as many as 100,000 or more nesting penguins.

One way to visualize a rookery is to think of it as a city, a city of penguins. Like any city, the rookery is broken up into communities. Penguin communities are called *colonies*, and they are usually separated from one another by at least a few yards. A very small colony contains only five or ten nests, whereas an extremely large one might contain as many as 10,000 nests. At Cape Hallet, where I studied adelie penguins, the average colony contains ninety-five nests. The nests, constructed entirely of stones, are very close together, giving the penguins just barely enough room to walk between them.

Skuas, which were mentioned earlier, nest around adelie penguin rookeries. They prey on adelie eggs and young adelie chicks, as well as scavenge for deserted eggs and dead chicks. Nesting in

Left: a coast guard cutter at Cape Hallet,
where many penguin colonies are located.
Cape Hallet is also where the author studied
penguins in Antarctica. Above: the skua,
a dangerous gull-like bird, often preys
on penguin eggs and chicks.

colonies gives the penguins good protection against skuas. Adult adelies are larger and stronger than skuas; any skua that dared enter a colony would soon be attacked and driven off. Most skuas, therefore, concentrate their efforts on stealing eggs and chicks at the edges of colonies, where the nests are less well protected. The safest sites for nests are those within the colony, not those on its edge.

One adelie penguin rookery in Antarctica is known to be about 650 years old. (Scientists determined its age using a technique known as radioactive carbon dating.) Some other rookeries are much older.

Let us consider now how adelie penguins returning to their breeding grounds after the long winter at sea go about establishing their cities, communities, and families.

To begin with, a migrating penguin may travel for weeks to reach its own home rookery. Other rookeries lying along its path are simply bypassed, even if they contain an abundance of suitable, unoccupied space. By marking birds with numbered bands, so that individual penguins can be recognized from one year to the next, scientists have learned that penguins who survive the winter will return to breed in the same rookery year after year.

The penguins usually arrive at their rookeries in October. This is spring in the southern hemisphere. Individuals that have bred before will in most cases return at once to the same colonies where they nested previously. There they will meet their mates. Birds arriving to breed for the first time will seek available nest sites and mates. Often the number of birds attempting to settle in a rookery is greater than the number of suitable nesting sites that are available. Consequently, many do not breed at all. However, after a penguin has bred for the first time, it will normally return to the same nest site and mate year after year. Hence penguins tend to be monogamous. However, some "divorces" and "remarriages" do occur. Also, a bird will seek a new mate if its old one fails to return to the colony for the breeding season.

If a male that has bred previously arrives and finds another male on his nest site, a fight ensues. Almost invariably the male that has used the site before wins the dispute. If a female arrives and finds another female with her male, she attacks the strange female and drives her off. Each pair of penguins goes through a period of courtship at the beginning of the breeding season. This occurs even if the pair has mated in previous years. Courtship is a matter of becoming acquainted or reacquainted before undertaking the serious business of fertilizing, laying, and incubating the eggs and rearing the young.

The nest site and a small area around it is defended by the owners. Biologists refer to such defended areas as *territories*. Both members of the nest work at gathering stones, which are piled up in the middle of the territory. After sufficient stones have been gathered, the pile is shaped into a nest for the two eggs that will be produced. The female lays the first egg and then, one to four days later, she lays the second. An average adelie penguin egg weighs 120 grams, which is about 2½ percent of the female's body weight. The eggs need to be incubated for about thirty-seven days before they will hatch.

By the time the eggs are laid, the females have been ashore for just slightly over two weeks. They then depart for the sea and leave the males to incubate the eggs alone for two weeks. During these two weeks at sea the females feed intensively on krill. This replenishes their fat stores and makes up for the weight lost in producing the eggs. Then they return to the colony and take a turn incubating the eggs while the males go to sea to feed for two weeks. By now the males have fasted for about six weeks. Both

An adelie penguin atop its nest,
incubating an egg. The pink area, visible
just above the egg, is called a *brood patch*.

sexes live exclusively on stored fat when they are on land. Before he leaves for sea, the male collects stones to add to the nest. Stones are in short supply and so they are often pilfered from other nests.

When the male returns from his two-week stint at sea, he relieves the female. He incubates the eggs for only about one week this time, then is relieved by the female. It is now time for the eggs to hatch. Some eggs hatch when the father is still incubating, others after the mother has taken over tending the nest.

Occasionally an egg is accidently knocked out of the nest. If it does not roll more than about 6 inches (15 cm) away, the parent penguin usually reaches out with its bill and rolls the egg back into the nest. In fact, this egg-retrieving response is so automatic that a penguin will roll egg after egg into its nest, even if the eggs are not its own. Eggs that roll more than 6 inches away are not retrieved.

The chick breaks its way out of the egg, or hatches, with the aid of a special structure on the bill called the egg tooth. Hatching takes twenty-four to forty-eight hours to complete. Both eggs in the nest hatch at about the same time. (A few nests have only one egg and hence hatch only one chick rather than the typical two.) After hatching, the egg tooth is no longer needed and it falls off within a few days. The baby penguin emerges from the egg fully clothed in a warm, fluffy coat of down feathers — warm and fluffy after it dries, that is, for the chick hatches soaking wet from having been emersed in fluids while in the egg.

Chicks are guarded constantly until they are three weeks old. During this time the parents take turns guarding the chicks and fetching them food from the sea. Young chicks left unguarded are often captured and eaten by skuas. They can also freeze to death, because penguins do not develop the ability to control their own body temperature until they are about fifteen days old.

Above: an adelie following its egg-retrieval instinct.
Right: an adelie pair greeting one another as one returns
from the sea and the other prepares to depart. The young
penguin can be seen nestled below its parents' feet.

The chicks have voracious appetites, demanding to be fed several times a day by the guarding parent. They are fed partially digested food regurgitated from the parent's stomach. On this diet they grow rapidly. By three weeks they are large enough to be left unattended, allowing both parents to go to sea to capture food for them.

At this point the chicks form groups called *creches*. They find safety in numbers from skuas and are also able to huddle together for warmth when necessary. There usually are a few adults around the creche who will attack any skua that comes near. But the chicks are also large enough by this time to defend themselves to some extent.

A problem that puzzled early explorers in Antarctica was how a parent could ever locate its own chick in the creche to feed it. In fact it was even believed by some that adult penguins did not necessarily feed their own chicks but fed any hungry chick. This idea was dispelled by scientists who marked adult and young penguins and found that parents normally feed only their own offspring.

When a parent of creche-age chicks returns to land with food, it approaches the creche and utters a peculiar and loud call. Almost immediately its own chicks, and often one or two others, run up and begin begging to be fed. At this point the parent bird often seems reluctant to feed any of the chicks, even its own. Instead, it may peck at all of them, then run away with the chicks in pursuit. This *feeding chase* serves to eliminate strange chicks. The adult may pause, call again, and peck strange chicks even harder than before. After all strange chicks have been eliminated, feeding occurs. Feed chases are shorter when only the adult's own young are present, but they occur nevertheless. Chicks return to the creche within an hour or two after being fed.

By the time they are seven weeks old the chicks start to resemble adults. They have their gray, fluffy, juvenile down feathers replaced by the sleek, scale-like, black and white feathers of adolescence and adulthood. The chicks begin leaving their creches and colonies and moving to adjacent beaches. They seem restless as they walk along the beaches and exercise their flippers. Parents may feed their chicks on the beach right up to the time the chicks leave. Finally, when about nine weeks old, the young go to sea. Their parents stay behind to molt. The young know how to swim and catch food without being taught. The breeding season is over.

BREEDING IN OTHER PENGUINS

The breeding habits of the emperor penguin differ in some remarkable ways from those of adelie penguins. For one thing, emperors breed during the Antarctic winter rather than in summer. Sometimes they breed on land, but more often they breed on sea ice along the coast. Egg laying follows a period of courtship and mating, as in the adelie. But emperor females lay only one egg, rather than the two that is normal for adelies. Instead of the mother and father taking turns incubating the egg, as adelies do, the emperor males do all, or nearly all, of the incubating. No nest is built. The male simply holds the egg between his feet and body as he stands upright on the ice.

Eggs are laid in early May. Then the females go to sea until about mid-July, when the eggs are hatching. Incubating takes about sixty-five days. This is nearly twice as long as for adelie eggs. Finally, the female returns from the sea. She emits a loud call by the huddle. The male responds by moving out of the huddle and uttering a call of his own. This tells his mate where he is. Now the mother takes over the care of the nearly hatched egg or newly hatched chick while the male goes to sea. She keeps the chick on

**A creche of restless adelie chicks
that have nearly completed their molt from
juvenile down to adult-type feathers.**

her feet, feeding it food from her own stomach and protecting it from the cold. Meanwhile, the male remains at sea for about four weeks, restoring his fat reserves. He returns again in August and the female makes her next trip to sea in search of food.

A healthy, well-fed chick starts showing signs of independence when it is about one month old. At first it exposes parts of its body to the outside world while staying sheltered against its parent. Then it begins making brief explorations off of its parent's feet. Finally the chick gets so large that it can hide no more than its head beneath the parent. Then it and other chicks in the creche are on their own to protect themselves from the cold. Like creche-age adelie chicks, young emperors huddle together to keep warm during unusually cold or stormy weather. In December, after they have exchanged their juvenile down for adult feathers, the young emperors go to sea. Now they are completely independent of their parents. However, they weigh only half as much as adults.

Breeding habits of king penguins are similar in some ways to those of emperor penguins. Here again only a single egg is produced and the egg is incubated between the body and feet of the parent penguin rather than in a nest. Unlike the emperor, however, king penguins breed in summer, not in winter, and they breed on land, not on ice. Also, both king parents share almost equally in the task of incubating the egg before it hatches. Actually, the male incubates slightly longer than the female. Young king penguins are fed by their parents for up to thirteen months. In winter, the chicks are fed only once every three or four weeks and may lose half of their body weight between feedings.

Females of the remaining fifteen species of penguins normally lay two (sometimes three) eggs. Some of these species, even though laying two eggs, will usually raise only one chick. Several species nest in the shelter of bushes, trees, or rocks. Some, such as the Magellanic penguin, dig their own burrows to nest in when no

The stately king penguin.

other shelter is available. Galapagos penguins sometimes dig their own burrows but usually nest in natural caves or caverns close to sea level.

A pair of king penguins normally breeds only twice every three years. Black-footed penguins and smaller species are more active. They breed twice a year. Most other species breed once per year. In the Galapagos penguin, about one pair in four breeds twice a year; the other pairs breed less frequently.

COLONIES AND NEST POSITION
IN ADELIE PENGUINS

During the breeding season, an adelie penguin's worst enemies on land are its predators — mainly the skuas — and other adelie penguins. Nesting in dense colonies as they do gives adelies protection against both kinds of enemies. Adelies are very aggressive toward skuas. They are also larger and stronger than the skuas. If a skua tries to enter a colony to steal eggs or chicks, it is attacked and driven off by the penguins. Thus, nesting close to others gives an adelie some protection because any penguins nearby will join the attack against their common enemy, the skua.

By the same token, adelies living together in a colony help protect each other against marauding penguins. Due to the shortage of nesting stones around colonies, adelies work very hard at stealing stones from one another's nests. But a stone thief has difficulty approaching any nest in a colony because the victim and all of the adelies nearby will attack any strange penguin even coming near. In addition to stone thieves, there are always some penguins around the colony who are not breeding and who seem to have nothing better to do than wander around picking fights. Hostile territory owners in the colony keep these delinquents on the move.

Only birds whose nests are completely surrounded by other nests get the maximum protection offered by colony life. A skua or a troublesome penguin cannot approach such a nest without be-

(35)

Black-footed penguins.

ing attacked. The owner of a nest located at the edge of a colony is not so fortunate. Although it has some help from adelies on the colony side of its nest, the other side is unprotected except by the owner. As a result, birds nesting at the edge of a colony lose more eggs and chicks to skuas and more stones to rock thieves than do penguins nesting within the colony.

Some adelies, probably less than one pair in five hundred, nest completely outside of colonies. Rather than being exposed on only one side, as birds on the colony edge are, these poor penguins can be attacked from any direction. They lose more eggs, chicks, and nest stones than do birds within or on the edges of colonies.

In the same way that nest position influences breeding success of individual pairs of penguins, the size and shape of a colony affects the success of the colony as a whole. This is because some colony sizes and shapes have more nests in vulnerable positions than others do. For example long, narrow colonies have a greater percentage of nests exposed to the outside than round colonies do. The worst situation would be one in which the nests were arranged in a single line, with every nest in the colony exposed to predators and stone thieves from outside of it.

Colony size is also very important. Consider, for example, two colonies of different sizes but about the same roundish shape. In such a case, the smaller colony would have a greater percentage of its nests on the edge than the larger one would. Thus the smaller colony would suffer a greater percentage of lost eggs, chicks, and stones than the larger one.

AGE AND SEX IN THE
YELLOW-EYED PENGUIN

The influence of age and sex on breeding habits of penguins is well illustrated by the yellow-eyed penguin. An ornithologist named Lancelot Richdale studied this species in New Zealand for eighteen years. By marking birds with numbered metal rings on their legs he was able to recognize individual penguins year after year. He marked many birds when they were still babies in the nest and therefore knew their exact ages.

Richdale discovered that most female yellow-eyed penguins start breeding when they are two or three years old, whereas males do not begin breeding until they are three or four. Older birds are more successful than younger ones at producing offspring. This is because older females lay more eggs and also because they hatch more of the eggs that are laid. Among two-year-old females, about 60 percent lay two eggs and about 40 percent lay only one egg. Among females three or more years old, more than 90 percent lay two eggs and fewer than 10 percent lay only one egg. Furthermore, only about 30 percent of the eggs laid by two-year-olds hatch, whereas 70 to 90 percent of eggs laid by older females hatch.

Many yellow-eyed penguins have the same mate year after year. Others change mates. In each of two pairs that Richdale studied, the mates were together for more than six years. Other birds had as many as five different mates in ten years. Some males would be mated one year but have no mate at all the next year. Although females always found mates, males often did not. During every breeding season, then, there were some males without mates in the colony.

UNEMPLOYED PENGUINS

Around every penguin breeding area there always are some penguins who do not have eggs or chicks when the others do. Ornithologists refer to these birds as being *unemployed*. They are unemployed for various reasons. Some have lost their eggs or chicks, some are too young to breed, others have either lost their mates or have been unsuccessful at obtaining mates. At Richdale's yellow-eyed penguin colony in New Zealand, about 38 percent of

(38)

the birds present were unemployed each breeding season. Yellow-eyed penguins that are unemployed because they have lost their eggs or chicks tend to separate from their mates and disappear from the colony.

Unemployed birds often cause much trouble in the colony. Unemployed adelie penguins steal nest stones, fight with nesting birds, and even attack chicks. Sometimes they roam through the rookery in groups, like gangs of hoodlums, harassing skuas as well as other penguins. Although they are useful to the rest of the penguin community by attacking skuas, most of their other activities are disruptive to the colony.

Emperor penguins who are unemployed interfere in the lives of other penguins in several ways. One is that they fight for possession of abandoned chicks and even kidnap chicks from their rightful parents. Chicks are often injured during the fighting. Kidnapped chicks are showered with attention for a few hours, then abandoned by their kidnappers. Unless their real parents find them, these kidnapped chicks die of starvation or exposure.

Unemployed emperors also stir up fights in the breeding ground by annoying other birds. Sometimes they go so far as to attempt by force to pair with penguins that already have mates. This always instigates a fight.

KEEPING COMPANY
Many unemployed penguins "keep company" with a member of the opposite sex. In the yellow-eyed penguin, 15 percent of the individuals who are present at the breeding area but do not breed keep company with another. Some such pairs build good nests, some make only feeble efforts at nest construction, and others merely occupy a "campsite" without attempting to make a nest at all. In yellow-eyed penguins males are more numerous than females. Females who do not actually breed at least keep company with a male. However, due to the shortage of females, many un-

employed males do not have the opportunity to keep company with a female. They are the true bachelors of the colony.

Most pairs that keep company break up and find new partners the next season. A few go back together the following year and breed. Thus, for some, keeping company might be considered a period of engagement.

SEX RATIOS
The numbers of one sex compared to numbers of the other is called a sex ratio. For example, if both sexes are present in equal numbers the sex ratio is said to be one to one (written 1:1). If females are twice as numerous as males the sex ratio is 2:1.

Most animals are born with a 1:1 sex ratio. As far as we know, this is true of penguins. However, in emperor penguins scientists have discovered that the sex ratio changes after birth. This is because more females than males survive the summer to return to their breeding colonies in winter. No one yet knows why, but it appears that about 10 percent fewer males than females return to the colonies. Put another way, for every ten females that breed one year and return to breed again the next year only nine males do so.

In yellow-eyed penguins the situation is reversed. Females die at a faster rate than males, with the result that more males than females return to the colony each breeding season. This is why the majority of unemployed yellow-eyed penguins are males.

the language of penguins

Humans communicate with one another verbally, by means of spoken languages in addition to a variety of nonverbal signals such as hand gestures, postures, facial expressions, and sounds other than speech. Although penguins do not have a verbal language, they do use many nonverbal signals to communicate simple information among themselves. These signals consist of combinations of postures, movements, and sounds. For example, adelie penguins greet one another by bowing, trumpeting, and waving their bills skyward. They threaten by raising the head feathers and staring sideways at the opponent or by opening the bill and pointing it at the opponent. A penguin that makes itself look smaller by pressing its feathers down when threatened is indicating that it does not want to fight. Parents call loudly to let their chicks in the creche know that they have arrived with food. Chicks can tell the calls of their own parents apart from those of other penguins. By touching its parent's bill with its own, a young penguin signals that it wants to be fed.

These kinds of signals communicate information about a penguin's intentions and needs. A penguin can signal that it is hungry, aggressive, submissive, seeking a mate, seeking its offspring, and so forth. But it cannot communicate concerning events that happened yesterday or that are going to happen tomorrow. As far as we know only humans can discuss past, present, future, and ideas.

unusual penguins

Penguins, like people, differ from one another in appearance and habits. Differences in appearance are great enough that in time a person can learn to recognize individual penguins on sight. In addition to these ordinary differences between individuals, a few penguins are born with very rare and unusual traits. Out of many thousands of adult and immature adelie penguins that I saw in

Adelie with an unusual crest
of white feathers on its head.

Antarctica, I noticed six that had particularly striking peculiarities. One chick had three legs, another had extra toes on each foot and a claw on one of its wings, and a third was partially white rather than uniformly gray like normal chicks. Among the adults, one had a beautiful crown of long white feathers on its head and another was black rather than white on its chest. Both of these birds were mated to normal penguins. A third unusual adult was not so lucky. Its entire back, instead of being black, was a pale creamy-shade, nearly white. This penguin tried constantly to associate with normal adults, but they would attack the poor bird and chase it away. A fourth adult was normal when it left the colony one day to fetch food at sea for its chicks. But when it returned one of its wings was missing, probably bitten off by a leopard seal. Despite her handicap, this penguin continued caring for her two chicks and fetching food from the sea for them. She and her mate successfully raised the chicks until they left for the sea, more than six weeks after her accident.

fossil penguins

The remains of plants and animals that have died are sometimes preserved in rock, where they can last millions of years. Such remains are called fossils and they provide us with a history of life on earth. By studying fossils scientists have learned that the first birds lived about 160 million years ago. They resembled feathery, flying lizards, if you can imagine such creatures. Over the next several million years many kinds of more advanced flying birds descended from these primitive ancestors. Among these flying birds were the ancestors of penguins. Penguins have lost the power of aerial flight (flying in air) possessed by their ancestors and specialized instead in aquatic flight (flying in water).

Dr. G. G. Simpson, an expert on fossil penguins, believes that the change from aerial to aquatic flight in the ancestors of penguins occurred more than 65 million years ago. It is clear from the fossil record that penguins already existed 45 million years ago and they have changed very little since then. Fossil penguins, like modern penguins, lived only in the southern hemisphere. At times in the past there were many more species of penguins than there are now, but most of them have become extinct. Among the extinct penguins are two that were quite large compared to living penguins. These were 5 feet 4 inches (1.6 m) to 5 feet 7 inches (1.7 m) tall and weighed about 300 pounds (135 kg). The largest living penguin is the emperor, which stands about 3 feet 3 inches (1 m) tall and has a maximum weight of about 100 pounds (45 kg). (The emperor's average weight is only 66 pounds, or 30 kg.)

comfort movements

Many activities of penguins and other birds are related to the care and comfort of their own bodies. Biologists call these activities *comfort movements.* They include such things as yawning, stretching, scratching, shaking, ruffling feathers, bathing, and preening.

Preening refers to the grooming of a bird's feathers with its beak. It is a very important activity because feathers must be properly groomed in order to keep the penguin warm and waterproof. In addition to simply arranging the feathers, penguins (and most other birds) also apply a coat of water-repellent oil to them while preening. This oil is produced by the preen gland, located beneath the feathers on the upper surface of the bird's tail. The penguin takes oil from this gland in its bill and rubs it onto the feathers. Feathers of the head and neck are oiled by rubbing these parts directly on the gland.

Penguins shake themselves frequently. First they ruffle up their feathers, then they vigorously shake their entire bodies. They do this to remove things from their feathers. They also do it any time the feathers are out of order, as it puts them back into the proper arrangement.

Penguins wash dirt out of their feathers by bathing in sea water. Penguins that have been ashore for a while have soiled feathers and are quite easy to distinguish from clean birds recently arrived from the sea.

fighting

Fighting is dangerous and costly. An animal may be wounded or even killed in combat. At the very least, fighting takes time and energy that could be devoted to more necessary activities such as eating, mating, nest-building, or preening. It is not surprising, therefore, that wild animals very rarely fight without good cause. Normally they fight to acquire or defend something such as a mate, a nest site, or food.

The willingness of a penguin to fight varies with its species, location, sex, and season. In adelie breeding colonies, for example, suitable space for nests and even stones with which to build nests are often in short supply. Adelies fight over nest sites and steal stones from one another. In general they are just very aggressive toward one another in the colonies. However, as individuals leave the colony to feed at sea they form peaceful groups. They become aggressive again upon returning to their nests.

(45)

Emperor penguins, on the other hand, breed mainly on ocean ice and do not build nests. Males may battle one another during competition for mates, but after that they have very little to fight over. Although some arguing and fighting goes on, the emperors' huddles are very peaceful compared to the adelies' colonies. If breeding emperors were as aggressive toward one another as breeding adelies are, they would not be able to huddle together for warmth while tending their eggs and young in winter blizzards.

When penguins fight they use their wings and bills as weapons. A penguin's flipper might not look like much of a weapon, but it is very effective. On numerous occasions I have received painful, walloping blows from the flippers of adelie penguins as I approached their nests. I have also seen one adelie strike another with such force as to send it reeling through the air.

penguins and humans

The oldest relationship between people and penguins probably was one of predator and prey. Natives of Tierra del Fuego, at the southern tip of South America, hunted penguins for their meat and skins. The Maori people first discovered New Zealand more than a thousand years ago and have lived there ever since. It is very likely that they ate penguins, though they no longer do so. Likewise, the original coastal inhabitants of southern Africa must have preyed on these plump, nourishing birds.

However, the greatest human predation on penguins started when Europeans arrived in the southern hemisphere. At first penguins and their eggs were taken to supply food for crews on sailing ships. Later the demand for meat and eggs increased as more and more ships visited the regions and as European settlements were established. Penguin skins began to be used for clothing, floor mats, and roofing. Their feathers were used to decorate women's clothing and to stuff pillows and mattresses. Large-scale commercial slaughter of penguins was underway. During the nineteenth century millions of penguins were killed to render their fat into oil and millions of penguin eggs were collected to supply food for settlements in and near southern Africa, New Zealand, and South America.

Although commercial hunting of penguins and their eggs has nearly stopped, some are still killed for their skins, feathers, and for use as fish bait. And in places like the Falkland Islands and the Tristan da Cunha Islands, penguin eggs are still collected for food.

NEW PREDATORS INTRODUCED
Humans have carried harmful predatory animals from other parts of the world into regions where penguins live and breed. Dogs have been imported nearly everywhere, even to Antarctica, where they kill and eat penguins. Cats, rats, stoats, and ferrets have been introduced in certain areas; they prey on penguin eggs and chicks and sometimes on adults. Pigs brought to the Tristan da Cunha Islands once destroyed an entire rookery of rockhopper penguins.

TRASH DUMPS
Several nations have built research stations in Antarctica. Refuse at these stations is a source of food for skuas. It allows areas around research stations to support more skuas than they would otherwise. In cases where penguins nest near the stations, the increased number of skuas seems to have resulted in increased attacks on penguin eggs and chicks.

Rockhopper penguins.

PESTICIDES

Chemicals used to kill insects and other pests are called pesticides. Farmers apply large quantities of pesticides to their fields to destroy insects that are harmful to crops. Pesticides are also used to control disease-carrying insects such as mosquitoes. These chemicals are eventually washed into rivers and carried to the sea. There they circulate through the world's oceans and concentrate in living plants and animals. Birds and other animals eating foods that contain pesticides build up these harmful substances in their bodies. When the concentration of poison in a bird's body reaches a high enough level, the bird either dies or becomes unable to reproduce. One effect of pesticides on birds is to cause eggshells to be so thin that they break when the birds attempt to incubate them. Peregrine falcons, brown pelicans, and other species have suffered from eggshell thinning. Pesticides are now so widespread in the oceans that even penguins in Antarctica are concentrating pesticides in their bodies. These penguins, located thousands of miles from areas where pesticides are heavily used, could have their reproduction reduced by our poisons.

The pesticides referred to are chlorinated hydrocarbons. DDT is an example. Since the harmful effects of these chemicals have been publicized their use has decreased, and they are now being replaced by less harmful poisons. However, they are still being used in many countries.

GUANO

Accumulations of bird droppings are called *guano*. Guano is a good fertilizer because it is rich in nitrogen, phosphorus, and other nutrients required by plants. Because of this, deposits of guano that accumulated over thousands of years on seabird islands have been dug up and carried away in the holds of ships.

Peruvian penguins in South America and black-footed penguins in South Africa once raised their young in caverns carved deep into guano deposits on their nesting islands. As guano was removed by humans, the penguins were dug out of house and home. With nest sites reduced, the number of penguins has also decreased.

Droppings of rockhopper penguins on Tristan da Cunha Island and droppings of Magellanic penguins in the Falkland Islands fertilize the tussock grass where these penguins nest. Because of this, the tussock grass, also known as penguin grass, grows better where penguins are present. Sheep farmers often feel kindly toward penguins because the grass fertilized by the penguins provides food for the sheep.

OIL SPILLS

We require oil to heat our homes, run our cars, and supply our other energy needs. Much of this oil is transported at sea in large ships called oil tankers. With increasing numbers of tankers operating at sea, the number of accidents they are involved in is also increasing. Wrecked tankers spill their oil onto the sea, where it can do great harm to penguins and other water birds. Thousands of penguins have been killed by oil spills in southern Africa and South America.

Even small amounts of oil can destroy the ability of feathers to keep a layer of warm air trapped around a bird's body. Oiled seabirds die of exposure, and the colder the sea the faster they die. It has also been discovered that small amounts of oil placed on eggs prevent the eggs from hatching. So a bird surviving some oil on its feathers might still kill its own eggs while incubating them. In addition, birds try to preen the oil off of their feathers with their bills. While doing so they swallow some oil. Scientists have found that ingested oil interferes with a bird's ability to produce healthy eggs.

WHALING

Seven species of baleen whales inhabit the seas around Antarctica. These include the blue whale, the largest animal that has ever lived. Instead of teeth, baleen whales have plates of baleen, or whalebone, hanging from the roofs of their mouths. Like adelie and chinstrap penguins, baleen whales feed mainly on the little shrimp called krill. They use their baleen to filter huge quantities of krill from the Antarctic seas.

Antarctic baleen whales have been hunted by humans until now most species are nearly extinct. Still, whalers from Japan and the Soviet Union continue to slaughter these great animals. Oddly enough, this senseless killing of whales may have benefits for penguins. With the whales disappearing there are more krill available for penguins to eat. Scientists estimate that the vanishing whales are freeing enough krill to feed 200 to 300 million more penguins each year. Both adelie and chinstrap penguins seem to be increasing as the whales decrease.

However, any advantage penguins have gained by the murder of whales may be short-lived. Even now plans are underway to begin the fishing of krill for human consumption. If the harvesting of krill is done as carelessly as the harvesting of whales has been, penguins may end up with less rather than more food.

epilogue

One day in Antarctica I was sitting alone next to an adelie penguin colony, relaxing and contemplating the society of penguins. I was delightfully awakened from my daydreaming when a penguin passing the colony ambled by within 2 feet (.6 m) of me, as if I were not even there. The adelie continued its absentminded journey for about 20 feet (6 m), then it suddenly stopped, turned around, and walked calmly back to me. It circled about me, looking me up and down. I had no way of knowing what went on in the mind of that penguin. However, I could not help wondering if the bird was not simply curious about me, just as I was curious about it and others of its kind.

Penguins have existed for many millions of years. During most of that immense span of time their major enemies have been in the sea. They had no really dangerous predators on land until humans started invading their domain, perhaps a thousand years or so ago. Consequently, until recently, penguins have had no reason to fear any animals on land. This is why they are so tame in the presence of humans and why it was so easy for hunters to kill them off by the hundreds of thousands. It is also the reason why penguins are exceptionally good subjects for the scientific study of wild birds. They are easy to approach, observe, and mark for recognition and they are not very disturbed by the biologists' intrusion into their lives.

And this is fortunate for us, for we still have much to learn from penguins.

bibliography

Benson, B. *The Penguin*. Cambridge: Cambridge University Press, 1978.

Boersma, P. D. "Adaptation of Galapagos Penguins for Life in Two Different Environments," in *The Biology of Penguins*, edited by Bernard Stonehouse, pp. 101–114, 1974.

——— "An Ecological and Behavioral Study of the Galapagos Penguin," in *The Living Bird*, Vol. 15, pp. 43–93, 1977.

Boswall, J., and MacIver, D. "The Magellanic Penguin *Spheniscus Magellanicus*," in *The Biology of Penguins*, edited by Bernard Stonehouse, pp. 271–305, 1974.

Emlen, John T., and Penney, Richard L. "The Navigation of Penguins," *Scientific American*, Vol. 215, pp. 104–113, 1966.

Herbert, C. F. "The Supraorbital Glands of Pygoscelid Penguins," in *The Biology of Penguins*, edited by Bernard Stonehouse, pp. 85–99, 1974.

Kooyman, G. L. "Behavior and Physiology of Diving," in *The Biology of Penguins*, edited by Bernard Stonehouse, pp. 115–137, 1974.

LeMaho, Yvon. "The Emperor Penguin: A Strategy to Live and Breed in the Cold," *American Scientist*, Vol. 65, pp. 680–693, 1977.

Maher, William J. "Predation's Impact on Penguins," *Natural History*, Vol. 75, pp. 42–51, 1966.

Murphy, Robert Cushman. *Oceanic Birds of South America, Vol. I*. New York: The Macmillan Co. (n.d.)

Penney, Richard L. "Territorial and Social Behavior in the Adelie Penguin," *Antarctic Research Series*, Vol. 12, pp. 83–131, 1968.

Richdale, L. E. *Sexual Behavior in Penguins*. Lawrence: University of Kansas Press, 1951.

Simpson, George Gaylord. *Penguins*. New Haven: Yale University Press, 1976.

Sladen, W. J. L. "The Pygoscelid Penguins," *Scientific Report of the Falkland Islands Dependencies Survey*, Vol. 17, pp. 1–97, 1958.

Spellerberg, I. F. "The Predators of Penguins," in *The Biology of Penguins*, edited by Bernard Stonehouse, pp. 413–434, 1974.

Spurr, E. B. "Communication in the Adelie Penguin," in *The Biology of Penguins*, edited by Bernard Stonehouse, pp. 449–501, 1974.

Stonehouse, Bernard, ed. *The Biology of Penguins*. New York: Macmillan Press, 1974.

——— *Penguins*. London: Bodley Head, 1978.

Tenaza, Richard. "Behavior and Nesting Success Relative to Nest Location in Adelie Penguins *(Pygoscelis Adeliae),*" *Condor*, Vol. 73, pp. 81–92, 1971.

Whitlock, R. *Penguins*. East Sussex: Wayland Publishers, 1977.

Young, P. *A Rare Bird in Antarctica*. Terry Hills, Australia: Reed, 1971.

index

*Page numbers in italic type
indicate illustrations.*

Adelie penguins, *3, 5, 6, 7, 8,
9, 14,* 17, *19, 20–21, 24–25,
26, 27, 28, 29, 30–31, 32,
35,* 37, *42, 45,* 51
Aquatic flight, *2, 3, 4*

Black-footed penguins, 35, *36,*
50
Blue shark as predator, 12
Blue whale, *9,* 51
Body temperature control,
13–14, *15,* 16–17, *18,* 20
Breeding habits of penguins,
*19, 20–21, 24–25, 26, 27,
28, 29, 30–31, 32, 33, 35,*
37–40

Cat as predator, 12, 47
Chicks, penguin, *19,* 27, *29,
30–31, 32*
Chinstrap penguins, 51
Colonies, *21,* 35, 37
Communications among
penguins, 30, 40–41

Cooling off methods, 16–17,
18
Countercurrent heat-exchange,
16
Creche, penguin, *30–31,* 32,
33

Diet, penguin, 4, 9, 11, 51
Dog as predator, 12, 47

Egg-retrieval instinct, 27, 28
Eggs, penguin, 25, *26, 27,
28, 31, 33*
Emperor penguins, *facing 1,*
*4, 5, 9, 11, 16, 17, 31,
33, 39, 40, 46*

Feathers, penguin, 14, *15,*
17, *18, 19,* 20, 32
Feeding chase, 30
Ferret as predator, 47
Fighting among penguins,
45–46
Food chain, 12–13
Fossils of penguins, 43–44
Fox as predator, 12
Fur seal as predator, 11

(57)

Galapagos penguins, 11, 35
Gentoo penguins, *15*
Giant petrel as predator, 12
Great auk, 1–2
Guano harvesting, 49–50
Gull as predator, 12

Hawk as predator, 12
Huddles, penguin, 16, 31
Humboldt's penguins, *18*

Incubation, 25, 26, 27, 31

Keeping warm, 13–14, *15*, 16, 20
Killer whale as predator, 12
King penguins, 17, 33, *34*, 35
Kooyman, Gerald, 5

Leopard seal as predator, 11–12
Lizard as predator, 12
Locomotion of penguins, 2, 3, 4–5, 6, 7, 8, 9

Magellanic penguins, 11, 33, 35, 50
Man as predator, 46–47, 51
Marauding penguins, 35, 37, 39
Migration of penguins, 9, 21, 24

Molting, 17, 20, 32
Monogamy among penguins, 24–25, 38

Nesting, 33, 35, 37

Octopus as predator, 12
Oil spills, 50

Penguin
    chicks, *19*, 27, 29, 30–31, 32
    creche, 30–31, *32*, 33
    diet, 4, 9, 11, 51
    eggs, 25, 26, 27, 28, 31, 33
    feathers, 14, *15*, 17, *18*, *19*, 20, 32
    huddles, 16, 31
Peruvian penguins, *10*, 11, 50
Pesticides, 49
Pig as predator, 47
Porpoising, 4–5
Predators, 11–12, 21, 23, 24, 35, 37, 39, 46–47, 51
Preening, 44–45

Range of penguins worldwide, 1
Rat as predator, 12, 47
Richdale, Lancelot, 37

(58)

Rockhopper penguins, 47, 48,
   50
Rookeries, 21, 24–25

Sacred ibis as predator, 12
Sally light-foot crab as
   predator, 12
Salt glands, 11
Sea eagle as predator, 12
Sea lion as predator, 11
Sex ratios among penguins, 40
Simpson, George Gaylord, 4,
   44
Skua as predator, 12, 21, 23,
   24, 35, 37, 39, 47

Stoat as predator, 47

Territories, 25
Tiger snake as predator, 12
Tobogganning, 5, 7
Trash dumps, 47

Unemployed penguins,
   behavior of, 38–40

Water rat as predator, 12
Whaling, 51

Yellow-eyed penguins, 37–38,
   39–40

about the author

Dr. Richard Tenaza is presently a professor of Ecology and Animal Behavior at the University of the Pacific in California. Dr. Tenaza has conducted research on the ecology and habits of birds and mammals in such places as Thailand, Malaysia, Indonesia, Antarctica, Alaska, and the Farallon Islands. He has served as a consultant to the United States government on problems of wildlife conservation in Alaska and has had many articles published on this and other subjects.